Editor-in-Chief and Founder:
  Lyndon H. LaRouche, Jr.
Editorial Board: *Lyndon H. LaRouche, Jr. , Helga
  Zepp-LaRouche, Paul Gallagher, Tony Papert,
  Gerald Rose, Dennis Small, Jeffrey Steinberg,
  William Wertz*
Co-Editors: *Paul Gallagher, Tony Papert*
Managing Editor: *Nancy Spannaus*
Technology: *Marsha Freeman*
Books: *Katherine Notley*
Ebooks: *Richard Burden*
Graphics: *Alan Yue*
Photos: *Stuart Lewis*
Circulation Manager: *Stanley Ezrol*

INTELLIGENCE DIRECTORS
Counterintelligence: *Jeffrey Steinberg, Michele
  Steinberg*
Economics: *John Hoefle, Marcia Merry Baker,
  Paul Gallagher*
History: *Anton Chaitkin*
Ibero-America: *Dennis Small*
Russia and Eastern Europe: *Rachel Douglas*
United States: *Debra Freeman*

INTERNATIONAL BUREAUS
Bogotá: *Miriam Redondo*
Berlin: *Rainer Apel*
Copenhagen: *Tom Gillesberg*
Houston: *Harley Schlanger*
Lima: *Sara Madueño*
Melbourne: *Robert Barwick*
Mexico City: *Gerardo Castilleja Chávez*
New Delhi: *Ramtanu Maitra*
Paris: *Christine Bierre*
Stockholm: *Ulf Sandmark*
United Nations, N.Y.C.: *Leni Rubinstein*
Washington, D.C.: *William Jones*
Wiesbaden: *Göran Haglund*

ON THE WEB
e-mail: eirns@larouchepub.com
www.larouchepub.com
www.executiveintelligencereview.com
www.larouchepub.com/eiw
Webmaster: *John Sigerson*
Assistant Webmaster: *George Hollis*
Editor, Arabic-language edition: *Hussein Askary*

EIR (ISSN 0273-6314) *is published weekly
(50 issues), by EIR News Service, Inc.,
P.O. Box 17390, Washington, D.C. 20041-0390.
(703) 777-9451*

European Headquarters: E.I.R. GmbH, Postfach
Bahnstrasse 9a, D-65205, Wiesbaden, Germany
Tel: 49-611-73650
Homepage: http://www.eirna.com
e-mail: eirna@eirna.com
Director: Georg Neudecker

Montreal, Canada: 514-461-1557

Denmark: EIR - Danmark, Sankt Knuds Vej 11,
basement left, DK-1903 Frederiksberg, Denmark.
Tel.: +45 35 43 60 40, Fax: +45 35 43 87 57. e-mail:
eirdk@hotmail.com.

Mexico City: EIR, Sor Juana Inés de la Cruz 242-2
Col. Agricultura C.P. 11360
Delegación M. Hidalgo, México D.F.
Tel. (5525) 5318-2301
eirmexico@gmail.com

Canada Post Publication Sales Agreement
#40683579

Postmaster: Send all address changes to *EIR*, P.O.
Box 17390, Washington, D.C. 20041-0390.

Signed articles in *EIR* represent the views of the
authors, and not necessarily those of the Editorial
Board.

Urgent Message To Congressmen

For Urgent Attention of Congressmen, Senators and Other Members of the U.S. Government

Oct. 5—Key responsible Congressmen and Senators (and there are some), and other U.S. government representatives must meet at once, to issue Findings of Fact and Statements of Commitment roughly as follows, for immediate enactment into law, and into immediate effect.

1. There is now an acute emergency which threatens to kill millions of Americans, primarily, and also citizens of other countries.

2. This is due immediately to the bankruptcy of Wall Street. Wall Street is totally and irremediably bankrupt. The successive Bush and Obama bailouts and the rounds of "quantitative easing," have only succeeded in making all of Wall Street's values valueless, and finalizing its bankruptcy.

3. If Wall Street is permitted to blow out again on its own terms, as now appears imminent, the result will be the worst panic in history, which will close down everything that remains of the U.S. economy. We will have mass death, on the order of the Black Plague which wiped out one-third

EIRNS/Stuart Lewis
U.S. Capitol Building, Washington, D.C.

of the population of Europe. Another Wall Street bailout, which Obama will demand if he is permitted to remain in office, would trigger a hyper-inflation just as deadly.

4. Hence, Wall Street must be closed down pre-emptively by U.S. Government action, in the spirit of what Franklin Roosevelt would do if he were alive today. (Although the crisis he faced was far milder.) Only activities compatible with a strict Glass-Steagall standard must be allowed to continue.

5. The Federal Government must issue U.S. dollars as credit to preserve the lives of the population and employ all the employable, in the spirit of Roosevelt's kindred actions with Harry Hopkins.

6. Over the slightly longer term, U.S. Federal credit must be used to rapidly raise the level of productivity of U.S. labor, through increased energy-flux density with scientific and technological progress.

7. Finally removing Barack Obama from office would be an excellent starting-point for these urgent reforms.

EIR Contents

www.larouchepub.com Volume 42, Number 40, October 9, 2015

Copy of an 1843 daguerreotype by Philip Haas

Cover This Week

John Quincy Adams wrote that he had achieved more as a Congressman 1833-1848, than earlier as President.

'The Government Must Shut Wall Street Immediately'

by Lyndon H. LaRouche, Jr.

This is Lyndon LaRouche's opening statement to the LaRouche PAC Policy Committee in Dialogue on October 5, 2015.

I've been pushing over the course of this weekend, the fact that we can no longer tolerate the risk which is involved in the renewal of Wall Street's conditions. And therefore, for that reason, we have to shut down Wall Street in order to protect the people of the United States. Because if Wall Street goes into another cycle of the type it just went through previously,—and it seems to be on the verge of it,—this means that the collapse of Wall Street, again, would result in a virtual sweeping-out of employment in many parts of the working population.

So therefore, apart from the fact that the crisis is there, we have Wall Street's condition, as opposed to the requirements of the people who are still employed, and families that are still involved,—and therefore we must take pre-emptive action.

What we've done, and what I've pushed for, is to have an immediate decision by relevant Members of the Congress, to assemble and deal with the situation as such. That was: foreclose against Wall Street without letting them get a bail-out effort. Because the giving of another option for bail-out to Wall Street would almost certainly ensure a great catastrophe of the people of the United States. In other words, the kind of breakout that we're on the edge of,—and these things are already serious enough,—means that you'll simply find there is no money to continue to pay the people who have been the employees on the El Cheapo scene.

So therefore we have to protect the population. We have to cancel Wall Street. And we have to proceed to restructure the organization of our employment for the intent of actually getting productive processes going

EIRNS/Stuart Lewis

Lyndon LaRouche, at his 93rd birthday party, Sept. 6, 2015.

into effect: essentially a more exigent sort of requirement than what Franklin Roosevelt had. But what Franklin Roosevelt suffered, and had to face and deal with, is minor compared to what this condition of the United States is right now.

This is combined with what's happening in Europe, what's happening in Germany, what's happening in France, in particular, in the relatively viable units. So therefore we've come to a condition where we actually have to say,—and I've been putting the word out,—that at this point, we must ask the Members of Congress who are relevant to act.

Now this is also a complicated thing, because we have a batch of new accomplices of treason, which is loaded into the Congress. We have people in the Congress who really are not serious people. They're bums. They should never have been, they're not really qualified to be Members of the Congress. And therefore, we have to take immediate action of that nature in order to secure the continuation of the U.S. as a nation,—that is, our national existence is now in jeopardy.

And the fact that we're operating largely on this basis, in our concentration on Manhattan, is extremely important as such. It's the one thing that must be done. It *is* the leading effort that must come on right now. If we do this, and if we get a number of serious Members of Congress, ones who really understand what this problem is,—and many of them do already have an inkling of what this is all about,—we have to say we have to act now to prevent a panic. It would really cause the kind of panic we don't want to even dream about.

And that's where we are. So therefore, we are in a situation where we've got to be absolutely merciless and shut down Wall Street, totally! They've got nothing coming to them except pain.

The Ban on Productivity-Increases And the Shooting of Ronald Reagan

by Jeffrey Steinberg

Oct. 6—In the background of the stark alternatives facing the U.S. economy today, is a ban on productivity increases which has been maintained since Franklin Roosevelt's death in 1945.

When programmed presidential assassin and Bush family associate John Hinckley shot Ronald Reagan, 70 days into the former California Governor's first term in the White House, the world changed, decisively, for the worse. President Reagan came into the Presidency in a landslide victory over the Trilateral Commission's Jimmy Carter in the 1980 election. He was committed to a revival of the American role in the world, starting with a revival of a U.S. economy that was beset by the consequences of the early onset of the Council on Foreign Relations policy of "controlled disintegration."

During the 1980 Presidential campaign, Lyndon LaRouche, who was running for the Democratic nomination against Carter, had powerfully injected a policy agenda into the race that addressed these concerns of Reagan and far more.

Reagan and LaRouche would go on to collaborate most publicly on the Strategic Defense Initiative (SDI), which aimed to bring an end to the era of thermonuclear terror through collaboration between the United States and the Soviet Union on technologies based on new physical principles, that would render thermonuclear weapons obsolete. But the areas of common interest were actually far broader.

LaRouche had featured his proposal for ballistic missile defense prominently in his Presidential primary campaigns, but had also produced a series of campaign white papers on such vital subjects as the revival of the North American Water and Power Alliance (NAWAPA).

EIRNS/Stuart Lewis

A promising start: President Reagan and Mexican President José López Portillo at a press conference in Washington, D.C. on June 9, 1981.

This was an integrated system of water management for the whole of North America, that had been originally designed during the 1960s by Parsons Engineering. NAWAPA was part of a larger economic "Grand Design" program, which featured plans to vastly expand and modernize the nation's vital infrastructure, revive the space program, complete the effort to achieve thermonuclear fusion power, and advance other areas of frontier science.

The Economic Promise

The LaRouche recovery plan began with a global debt moratorium and write-off, to end the tyranny against the developing world by the IMF and other agencies of world financial domination in the aftermath of the 1971 elimination of the Bretton Woods System of

Franklin Roosevelt. LaRouche called for the abolition of the Federal Reserve System, and its replacement by Hamiltonian national banking and Federal credit.

Although Ronald Reagan was a free-market conservative surrounded by advisors from the Austrian School of Friedrich Von Hayek and Milton Friedman, Reagan had also, at one time, been an FDR supporter and President of the Screen Actors Guild during his days in Hollywood. Above all else, Reagan was a patriot, who instinctively put the interests of the nation above ideological dogmas.

It was this deep personal character that ultimately attracted Reagan to the policies and principles of LaRouche. Through a close California friend, Reagan had been introduced to LaRouche's writings and to the *Executive Intelligence Review* (*EIR*),—whose pages you are now reading,—during his period as Governor of California. For half a decade before his 1980 Presidential run, Reagan had received the weekly *EIR* at his California ranch.

LaRouche and Reagan met in person for the first and only time in February 1980 during the bipartisan Manchester, New Hampshire Presidential debates sponsored by the National Rifle Association. The two men were seated next to each other on the corner of the stage and had hours to talk.

From the day that Ronald Reagan was elected President, he regularly ordered aides to sound out LaRouche on the most pressing and controversial issues which confronted him.

During the Presidential transition, LaRouche had publicly called for a face-to-face informal summit meeting between the U.S. President-elect and Mexican President José López Portillo to discuss mutual cooperation on economic development, which would ease tensions and effectively serve as a model for development of lesser developed nations. The two men did in fact meet before Reagan's inauguration. LaRouche was also called in to participate in transition team deliberations on domestic infrastructure.

The Bush Factor

Early in the Reagan presidency, before his near-assassination, Reagan was seriously contemplating an

Bush Presidential Library and Museum

Vice President George H.W. Bush on Air Force Two watching a replay of the assassination attempt against President Reagan.

overhaul of the U.S. Federal Reserve. He seriously considered firing Fed Chairman Paul Volcker, who had brought the U.S. economy crashing down by his 20% interest rate policies, which nearly wiped out the U.S. agricultural sector, and brought all investment in manufacturing and R&D to a screeching halt.

LaRouche not only backed the idea, he spelled out a plan for the elimination of the Fed, the creation of a Third National Bank, and the launching of the greatest expansion in capital-intensive job creation and infrastructure modernization since FDR.

Members of the Reagan inner circle were studying the LaRouche proposals, when Chase Manhattan Bank's David Rockefeller, the founder of the Trilateral Commission, stormed into Washington and threatened to bring down the entire U.S. economy if any move was made to dump Volcker.

Rockefeller was ultimately bluffing. Had the Reagan Administration adopted the LaRouche proposals, Wall Street would have been brought down, but the real U.S. economy would have gone through a recovery, and the tyranny of the London monetarist system would have been brought to an end.

President Reagan survived the Hinckley assassination attempt, but only barely. He would never fully recover, and, as the result, the bulk of the Reagan Presidency was a compromise between Reagan's patriotic gut-feelings, and the very Trilateral Commission oligarchy that he personally hated and had campaigned to remove from power.

The man who personified the Trilateralists' penetration and subversion of the Reagan presidency was Vice President George Herbert Walker Bush.

It took an extraordinary intervention at the 1980 Republican nominating convention to insert Bush into the Reagan Presidential slate. Reagan had personally chosen his close friend Sen. Paul Laxalt (R-Nev.) to be his running mate. But a vicious media campaign against Laxalt succeeded in blocking Reagan from putting Laxalt on the slate. Reagan was excoriated that he had to "balance" the ticket by selecting a running mate acceptable to Wall Street and the Eastern Liberal Establishment.

The decision remained frozen well into the GOP nominating convention. At one point, nominee Reagan was pressed to accept a "dual presidency" with Gerald Ford, the very Republican President who had been defeated by Jimmy Carter, and who had never been elected to the Presidency by the American people. Reagan's "kitchen cabinet" balked at the idea of surrendering Presidential powers to Ford.

What the Reaganites did not realize at the time was that this Ford ploy was a trap, aimed at getting Reagan to accept George H.W. Bush as his running mate. Bush's campaign had been totally crushed in New Hampshire, when Reagan beat him in the first primary election, right in the Bush family's back yard (the official family compound was located next door in Kennebunkport, Maine).

Bush was viewed by the Reagan inner circle as a weak figure, whose political career had been advanced by a series of appointive posts, and who had only served a few terms as a back-bench Republican Congressman from Houston. They clearly had not studied the murderous history of the Bush clan, including the role of George's father Prescott Bush in installing Hitler into power, and profiteering off of trading with the Nazi enemy.

Bush was chosen by Reagan as the "lesser evil," but along with Bush came a parade of Trilateral Commission and other rotten elements, who were ready to pounce the moment Reagan showed any sign of weakness.

Illustrative of the Bush subversion of the Reagan Presidency was the role of Bush's alter-ego, James Baker III, who, as White House Chief of Staff in March 1983, tried to suppress Reagan's crowning achievement as President—his March 23, 1983 SDI speech. On the day of the speech, Baker had ripped out the final three minutes of the Reagan speech, where the President was to launch the Strategic Defense Initiative to the Soviets. It was only because Reagan's National Security Advisor, Judge William Clark, who was dedicated to the SDI policy, bypassed Baker to get the com-

plete speech draft onto the President's desk for his approval, that March 23, 1983 went down in history as the launching of the SDI. Indeed, it was a world-historic moment.

In a 1982 year-end address to a national conference of his political movement in Manhattan, Lyndon LaRouche had said the world had reached a "punctum saliens" where mankind would either enact radical policy changes, or face an existential crisis. LaRouche demanded that President Reagan publicly endorse the SDI within the next 90 days, and also adopt LaRouche's debt moratorium, and his policy of return to national banking. LaRouche called for a total mobilization to achieve these goals.

Reagan's March 23, 1983 SDI speech fulfilled one of those two urgent policy goals. But the Bush League advisors had captured control of the Administration's economic and monetary policy, and Vice President Bush became the Reagan team's "privatization czar."

The Consequences

When Ronald Reagan first came into office, he held out the prospect of reversing the controlled disintegration, outsourcing, and radical monetarist policies of the Trilateral Commission's Carter Administration.

From the time of the death of President Franklin Roosevelt, right up to the present moment, the United States has gone through a continuing net decline in real productivity. True, there were exceptional moments, like President Dwight David Eisenhower's "Atoms for Peace," and President John F. Kennedy's Apollo program and his investment tax credits. Once JFK was assassinated and Lyndon Johnson was drawn into the Indo-China War, it was all over. Real productivity, as measured in Lyndon LaRouche's two physical economic principles—potential relative population density and energy flux density—has been on a downward spiral.

Reagan, with the active collaboration of Lyndon LaRouche, had a chance to reverse the collapse of productivity and launch a genuine recovery of the real economy. Reagan alone could never have done it, despite his genuine good intentions. But Reagan aligned with LaRouche was a different story, and had a real shot at restoring the nation's true values and history.

The assassin's bullets proved not to be physically fatal; but they were fatal to the opportunity of January 1981, and that is the proper point of reference for the lost opportunity to restore the true American system of economy.

Putin Has Acted, and the Existence Of Mankind Has Changed

Here are edited excerpts from Lyndon LaRouche's October 3 Dialogue with the Manhattan Project.

Dennis Speed: My name is Dennis Speed. On behalf of the LaRouche Political Action Committee I want to welcome everybody here, today. Today concludes the last fourteen heads of state speaking at the United Nations. I think everybody here certainly knows we've been involved in a full week of intervention there. And there were some decisive changes in the world that occurred, and those changes are not yet conclusive.

I want to go directly to Lyn and ask him if he has an opening statement for us, an evaluation of where we stand. Then that will be followed immediately by our questions. So, Lyn.

LaRouche: Yes, I just have one thing to say, because it's important to put this on the agenda so that the entire body here can get some sense of what has to be done in terms of practice. We have now just completed this program, which was intended for this event in Manhattan, but now we come to a new era which has already started. President Putin has actually instituted an action which is a rather complicated one relative to previous kinds of experience, in which he's acted to destroy a force of evil which is responsible for much of the problems which mankind, especially in Europe, in particular, is suffering at this time. And therefore we will find that the things have changed from the standards of what we would have had a week ago. Because we've entered a new period of civilization in this form.

And therefore in what I shall do in responding, as

President Vladimir Putin, with his moves in Syria, has acted to destroy a force of evil. Here, he confers with Russian Defense Minister Sergei Shoigu at the conclusion of a military exercise on Sept. 19, 2015.

the questions come up,—I shall bring into effect different kinds of responses, not essentially different, but different in the sense of the way I approach matters now. Because what's happened is that the entire existence of mankind living in all parts of society has changed. It changed this week, in the course of the end of this week, and therefore we have to keep our minds open to reflect on what the new condition is, which has just been established and introduced today.

Q: Hi, Mr. LaRouche, it's H__ from Bronx, New York. I just want to talk a little bit about the events of this week. We had a major rally on Monday on 42nd Street. I think we got a tremendous amount of attention. I'm paraphrasing some of these things, but we had a big banner: "Obama, Help Peace, Resign!" We were getting people who were enthusiastic about Obama resigning. We had some supporters of Putin's shift, on fighting ISIS. So, I think we were getting a very big response

8   Urgent Message to Congress

EIR   October 9, 2015

in changing the atmosphere.

Throw Out Obama with Wall Street

And then also on Thursday, myself and my wife,—who's a Spanish speaker,—we intervened at an event where the President of Paraguay was speaking at NYU [New York University], which was a little bit difficult for me, because even though it was NYU, everybody was speaking Spanish in the event. I know a little bit of Spanish, but I tried to do the best that I could.

Anyway, we got a question to the President of Paraguay,— Paraguay down between Brazil and Argentina. His name is Horacio Cartes. He was speaking about various things: about the development of Paraguay, about getting some students to go to NYU and other of these wonderful schools we have up here. We had a question on a piece of paper that we didn't know if it would go through, but it went through to the moderator who is a former Foreign Minister of Mexico, Mr. Casteñeda, and the question was: "What do you, the President of Paraguay, think Paraguay can do with the help of the BRICS bank, to increase the investment in the infrastructure in Paraguay?"

We immediately created a stir in the room, of restlessness, because this was obviously not on the program of the people at NYU,—thinking about how the BRICS bank was going to change Paraguay or the world. The President said, well, he thought this was interesting; and then he went through—let's see, what are the BRICS? Brazil, Russia; and then someone told him about China. Then he remembered that Paraguay, like certain countries in Central America, doesn't even have relations with mainland China right now; they still have relations with only Taiwan. So, Paraguay really does not have any diplomatic relations with China at all, even though he was interested in the role of the BRICS. Obviously, Brazil is right next door.

So he did refer this question to his Foreign Minister, and after the presentation, me and my wife got the *EIR* magazine about the reforms of Franklin Roosevelt to

White House/Pete Souza

Obama, "a servant of Satan in effect," in the Oval Office on Aug. 8, 2015.

the Foreign Minister, who also was familiar with your work, Mr. LaRouche.

I don't really have a question, but I see that we are beginning to get the message that things have changed in the world to some people, who are very slowly waking up. I don't know if we can make them wake up a little faster, but that's what we're doing.

LaRouche: Okay, well, I can say something on this subject, which is probably useful for what you just said. The point is that what happened is that suddenly Obama was being dumped from the Presidency of the United States. Now, the *fait accompli* has not arrived, but the situation of Obama is now new and crucial. If he were to remain as President, that would be a tragedy for all mankind. He would actually be a *threat* to most of mankind in every part of the planet.

So, this actually is the issue that's hot right now. Obama must be thrown out of office, along with Wall Street. Now, Wall Street is totally bankrupt. It has no ability to function any more. It's part of the walking dead; that's the best way to describe what this thing means. So therefore, what happened with Putin is that Putin acted, not in a sense of an ordinary way we would interpret it. Putin actually moved *to destroy evil*. And he's done a fairly good job in the initial progress of what he's done, but this is not a war run by Putin because of some grievance that he has.

What he's done, what he's doing, is supporting the

bringing together of nations of both the European region, and below Europe,— across in Africa and so forth,—in their attempt to clean up Satan, get rid of Satan. And the view is, as I can tell you if you want to argue that, that Obama is a child of Satan. And that's what the problem is, and therefore lots of people around this planet *now* have recognized this fact, and they are acting not to slaughter somebody, but in order to destroy Satan, i.e., in this case, Obama and his friends.

Q: Hello, Mr. LaRouche. I am S__ from the New York area and my question is: Last week the president of Argentina called President Obama a traitor. And I would like to know what is the strategic importance of that statement? And I also have a question after that.

LaRouche: Well, Obama is actually a kind of Satan, explicitly. The point is, how are we going to deal with this guy, bring him under control and prevent him from becoming successfully Satanic? In other words, we're trying to change the way the world has worked for some recent times, and this is trying to create a new option for mankind. This means defending mankind, getting rid of real evil, things that have been destroying... For example, we have in Europe a very large number of people coming into Europe, who are fugitives from Obama and Obama's associates. That's the problem.

Obama and the Mass Shootings

So what Putin is doing,—he's undertaken the responsibility of getting Obama out of the picture. This is not an attack on Obama; it's getting rid of him. Because the man is actually evil, has been evil from the first time he moved. Also his stepfather was the guy who taught him how to be *evil*. And he came into the United States as an evil person from the first time he walked in there. He was already a servant of Satan in effect. That's the way people would say it, and that's what he represents. He was a destructive, purely defective kind of force, and the time has come to get rid of him. Put him out of office.

And the purpose of this process which Putin is playing a key role in, momentarily at this time, is to get rid

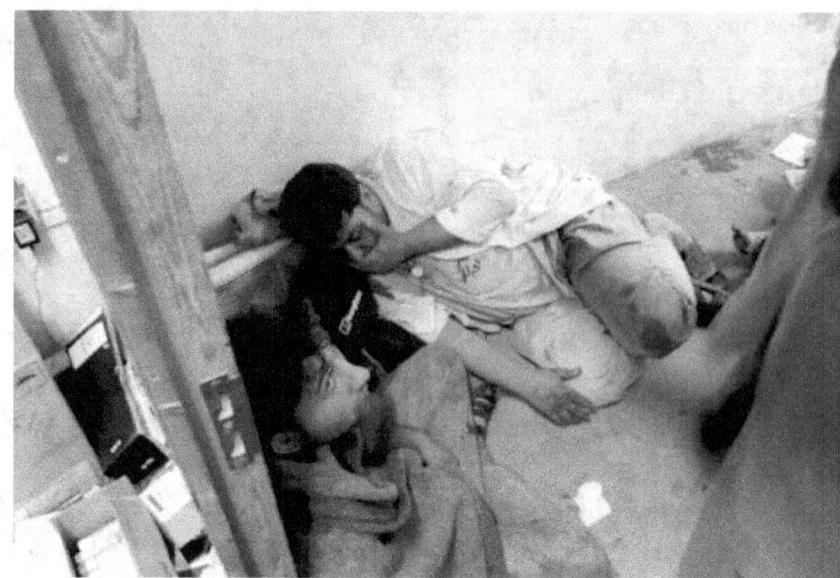

Doctors Without Borders

Doctors react to the U.S. airstrike on their hospital in Kunduz, Afghanistan on Oct. 3.

of the kind of warfare and destruction which mankind has suffered too long. This is to clean up the mess, not to win a war.

Q: Hi, Lyn, it's A__ again. What I'm wondering about is being,—perhaps not distracted,—but finding myself drawn in, because even after the Thursday call, now we see the shooting in Oregon,—you know, another mass killing. And people are concerned about this, and it's valid. And then you have in Afghanistan a bombing.

And it's very simple, yet dangerous to start making assessments and discussing these things. Keeping this lifeline and dialogue with you is very important. Even in New York City now, just because there's a storm that is pending, people are panicking,—those who are living in those vulnerable areas where, of course, nothing's been done.

So, as an organization, I think we can be pulled apart in trying to think clearly and stay on the ball. So, these self-assessments I think can be dangerous and sidetracking; how must we think or proceed to remain with what we must stay focussed on?

LaRouche: Let's take the most recent case of a shooter, a gun-shooter; what's that represent? This is not some guy who "did" something; yes, he did do something, but what caused these kinds of actions recently? Well, it wasn't caused by one person; it wasn't caused by *a* person as such. Not in a pattern like that, no. The gun-shooting, a lot of the recent things, are part of the Obama Administration, they're a product of this process.

Now Obama is not the creator of this, but he certainly is a fosterer of it. And therefore, the problem is, we've got to get some degree of control over the process, because we have a lot of people who are eligible to be murderers. The increase of the murderer population is accelerating, and it's not happening accidentally. It's happening. It may be induced by somebody who doesn't know what he's being induced to do.

But this is a new pattern; it's a threat to humanity. And you have to remember that what Obama represents is the reduction of the human population. And therefore what you're seeing is an effect which is the reduction of the human population. That's what you're looking at. And this is a process which has a systemic characteristic to it. This is not just one guy shooting some people up. When this pattern is repeated in the same way, again and again and again, as it's been doing recently,— we've had these patterns before, but this is the most serious period.

And the problem lies inside,—I think you could say, not that Obama did these killings, but that what his behavior did was contribute to that kind of phenomenon. And we have a society,—look, we have a society which no longer has morals, in general; not real morals. Look at people who don't have income; look at the number of people who are being deprived of income; look at the number of people who are being deprived of everything that's important to them, demoralizing our citizens, especially younger people.

And this is the pattern. It's a pattern of evil. And it comes from a characteristic that our government, especially the Bush and the Obama Administrations, are exemplary of forces of evil! That's what they've done. And I know a lot of the detail of both of these administrations, and however witting they are, or non-witting they are, their actions, their outlook, is one of evil,—it has been.

And that's what you have to worry about. We have to take the actions to requalify our own citizens, to ensure that the population as such, becomes more productive, and less destructive.

Putin an Instrument for Civilization

Q: Hello, Mr. LaRouche, it's a pleasure talking to you. My name is L__. I am from Italy, although I've been living here a few years. My question for you is to ask your consideration about the situation in Europe, especially in terms of how the diplomacy is developing in the clash between Russia and the United States and NATO, and the appearance of it developing as a sort of new cold war.

So I just wrote down a couple of things that will lead me to my question for you. Basically, the situation is that the tide of consensus in Europe, but also worldwide, at least from the point of view of common people, is constantly growing in favor of Putin and Russia. And some signs of reversion from sheer acceptance of U.S. orders in terms of diplomacy and financial organization of our nations, seem to be taking place among some politicians. I'm thinking most importantly about Hungary and [Prime Minister] Viktor Orban, for example, who unfortunately, I think, may be about to experience a color revolution coming his way soon. We hope not, but that's a risk, and maybe you can give me some considerations on that, too.

But my question for you is: Do you see any room for an effective change of policies on the part of European governments in terms of joining that popular tide in favor of Russia, and thus start building a strategy that can liberate us as Europeans from this,—I would define it as servitude,—that has been established after the end of the Second World War, and even more strongly after the fall of the Berlin Wall?

LaRouche: I would say the real point today, is that the future of mankind,—as opposed to what has been the immediate earlier period,—is that what Putin was prompted to do, and I emphasize prompted to do, because Putin did not act on his own, in terms of what he did. He acted on the basis of a relationship within the European system, and within India, Indian society, in China, and so forth. So this was a joint effort in which Putin performed a function corresponding to the perceived interests of a whole part of [world society].

Now the corruption of Spain, Italy, and so forth, was a product of the failure to solve this problem. Mostly, it was done by the British. The British Empire was really the vehicle of orchestration to ruin Europe and to reduce other parts of the world. It was a colonial system; it was an evil system, a Satanic system, essentially, at root. And so this was the problem.

Now what's happened is that Europe has come to realize—more and more parts of Europe or people within Europe—have come to realize that that was all wrong. And they're looking for solutions in order to reconstruct the economy, the functional economy, and social conditions of life which are necessary,—which

kremlin.ru

"Putin has become an instrument on behalf of civilization." Here, he is shown with his close partner Chinese President Xi Jinping during the Ufa BRICS Summit, July 8, 2015.

are, for example, the education of our people. The educational system in most parts of the world is deteriorated greatly, as in Europe generally.

So that what's happened here: The process here is that Putin has become an instrument of his own self; he's made himself his own instrument on behalf of civilization, for Russia, and for other people, as well. And so, most recently, what he's done, he went in there to save citizens in that area, and also to get rid of some of the pestilences which were mass murdering, so as to bring a peaceful order. And Putin has worked closely with China, worked closely with India, worked closely with people of other BRICS nations as well, and so these are forces that had to be brought together in concert, to a concert of agreement in order to get a decent kind of new peace for mankind.

Now peace is not submission. Peace is the ability to be actively efficient in bringing mankind to reach the opportunities for success of mankind's development. And this is true of every part of the world; you know it from the standpoint of Italy, and the fact of the conflicts which existed inside Italy's culture, where certain parts were one thing and certain were another.

The time has come that we've got to bring a resolution among all nations if we can, into coming to an understanding of what the nation is, what the function of the nation is, and to understand that the different na-

tions require the ability to access that function. We need a revolution in thinking. And the time has come, I think, that we may get it. I think we may succeed. I know the opportunity for success is there, and of course, I will do what I can about that myself.

But I say,—don't be pessimistic about this thing. I think great opportunities are being given to us—opportunities we've missed for a very long time. Get rid of Wall Street, for example. That's one of the good things we're going to do.

We Can Do What FDR Did

Q: Good afternoon, thank you for taking my question. My name is M__ B__. I was watching something on RT [news broadcaster] about—it was a sort of Noam Chomsky type character from Slovenia; and when he was watching the speeches in the UN, in particular Poroshenko and Obama and Putin, he got this flashback from his Russian childhood days of Russian TV, of a Bugs Bunny type character they had in Russia, saying "What's going on here? What's this about?" Because everyone's talking rationally, but they're throwing barbs at each other.

But what he did say,—one troubling thought that came to him,—was that he sees this happening more and more in the world. Like Ukraine will become yet another place in the world where there will be a soft peace without any kind of unified state power structure, and it will just go on like Lebanon. Lebanon, of course, after the civil war, never became an effective state any more, but they did manage to succeed economically. And he sees this is happening all the time now in other parts of the world.

So, it would be just an endless cycle of some shooting, then an armistice, but nothing really serious, but it'll be—it's the strategy of tension in action, that whole neo-con ideal. So what thoughts do you have on this, and can you add anything to that that we should be thinking about?

LaRouche: Right now, the danger is,—take the U.S. population as such. The U.S. population is now threatened by accelerating rates of death; it's not necessary, but what's happening is, you have more and more of the population of the so-called unemployed people, who are losing everything they had in terms of assets, again and again and again.

National Archives/Ann Rosener

Franklin Roosevelt's actions served to organize the U.S. population back to productivity. The skills these workers in the Willow Run Ford plant developed building a bomber, prepared them to rebuild the economy after the war.

So now, if the United States were to go into a depression, a classical type of U.S. depression, now, the death rate inside the United States would be enormous. The only way that we could solve that problem is as an emergency, because we are not able, under the present financial system, to maintain a healthy population, and a productive population at all. People are being dumped like rubbish, in effect, into the job loss and conditions of deteriorating production and employment.

So we're now at a point where it's extremely important that we take action to put in a Franklin Roosevelt action, of the type that Franklin Roosevelt applied to the Depression in the 1930s. Without that kind of action, and without also dumping and closing down all Wall Street institutions, there's no chance of defending humanity safely. That's what the problem is.

In other words, shut down Wall Street! First thing! Wall Street is dead. It cannot possibly develop anything positive. It's hyperinflationary, it has no productive characteristics any more; so therefore, we have to remove it. If it won't remove itself, we'll have to remove it.

But on the other hand, we don't have a mechanism now to provide an employment program of the type which would allow us to reconstruct some of the productivity of our people who are being raped, essen-

tially,—being starved of every right they have. It's an emergency situation: If we went to a Franklin Roosevelt approach of the 1930s, and said we're going to suppress this, and we're going to back this,— and we're going to provide provision, to get the population organized to rise back to productivity,—what Franklin Roosevelt did from the time he became President, until the time he died. Franklin Roosevelt had created a great movement of progress for mankind in the case of the United States, but also what the United States did internationally.

And what we have to do is say that what Franklin Roosevelt contributed to a nation's economy which was not working,—Franklin Roosevelt's approach is the correct one, and with that approach we can improve the education, for example. What my experience is,—you know, I'm not the youngest man by any means, on this planet, but I went through all these experiences as a young person, and we developed in the course of my experience; we increased the productive powers of labor of the members of the United States' population. We improved that! We made great improvements in terms of technology under wartime conditions and even prewar conditions.

We Can Fix the Problem!

We can do that again! But we must get Wall Street shut down! Because if Wall Street were to go any further in a collapse, there would be no support for the categories of citizens of the United States who have no protection, economic protection. They'll be on the street! They'll be dead; starved. So it's important that we get rid of Wall Street. Shut it down because it's worthless. But as long as Wall Street and the members of Congress who support Wall Street,—as long as they're doing what they're doing, most of the people of the United States are threatened by a very serious destruction of their right to life.

And so therefore we've come to the time that getting rid of Obama, throwing him out, and following the trail which Putin and which Germany, are doing, in particular, and China, and India,—follow that route, make

creative commons/Gregroy Hausensteing

creative commons, AFGE

Democratic Presidential candidate Martin O'Malley (left) and Senator Elizabeth Warren (right) are campaigning for restoring Glass-Steagall.

sure we do it! And we can survive.

But we've come to a time where we're on a short leash! We don't have a long leash for dealing with this thing; we've got to do it quick. And I think that you'll find that the UN conference, which was just in process here,—that thing is going to be a natural supporter of the kind of reform among nations, among whole groups of nations,—maybe not all nations, but whole groups of nations,—is going to do something to change the way the world has functioned in the short term, up to now.

Speed: I think those are the last of our questions, and you already began to touch on what I was going to ask you for our conclusion. Because it's this: We seem to have accomplished as a result of the process you started last June, late June, a rejection of Obama internationally: you defined how the United Nations process was doing, and what happened was, we took a force in Manhattan,—sure we had people nationally, but it was focussed here,—and we deployed as I believe you wished us to do. I could have you give us an evaluation of how you think we did on that,—but we've got a rejection of Obama internationally. Now we need a rejection of Obama nationally.

And what I want you to tell us, is how you want this crew, and our expanding forces who are also out here,—how do we deploy here now, using your idea about shutting down Wall Street and your idea about the Hamiltonian Presidency: What do we do here to advance that process?

LaRouche: We have to get Obama under control. That means even before we throw him out formally,

we've got to bring him under restraint. If we do that, and we can put Wall Street under constraint,—and if we can get some members of the Congress who are worse than idiots, and get them also discouraged from continuing to serve,—we could probably do a pretty good job of trying to rebuild the U.S. economy and the conditions of life which that represents. That's what the real solution is.

That's an approximation, but what I'm concerned about is, imagine that if Wall Street continues to become the instrument which controls the mind of the Congress, or the leading elements of the Congress, we are in *real, deep trouble*, or our entire population is deep trouble. Therefore, we must get rid of Obama's ability to control the U.S. government in any respect; and we have to take steps which ensure that we will not have a collapse of the income generation of our citizens. We have a situation of absolute desperation in the greatest part of our population! Most people don't realize how serious this is. The financial conditions, the economic conditions, of people in the nation, are terrible! And it's become worse at an accelerating rate.

Now, we can with a Franklin Roosevelt approach, we can fix that problem, despite all it represents. And I think that's what we have to do: We have to force the United States government, the agencies of government, to realize that they have a responsibility to deal with the sins, the evil sins, that the Congress in large degree has supported, by recklessness, by stupidity, by cupidity and so forth,—all these kinds of nice evil things. And we have to protect the population of the United States. We have to protect the *people* of the United States, the children of the United States. We've got to defend our population and its ability to think, its ability to create, its ability to achieve.

And we've got to end the regime which is typified by the name of Bush and the name of Obama.

Speed: All right, Lyn, thank you very much. I think that was quite clear. And we're going to get to work on that, and we'll see you next week.

LaRouche: À bientôt!

How Obama Learned to Love Murder

Oct. 6—No halfway-informed American can have missed Obama's gleeful delight in murder. Don't they know of his murder-targetting sessions every Tuesday in the White House, when Obama chooses the targets for the next week's drone-killings around the world,—from what he jokingly calls the "baseball cards" of the week's potential victims? Remember Hillary Clinton's public glee over the televised torture-murder of Libya's President Qaddafi in 2011, on Obama's orders, where she grinned triumphantly to an interviewer, "We came, we saw, he died?" As a terrorized victim-accomplice of Obama,—which is what she is to this day,—Hillary was just mindlessly echoing-back her sadistic boss.

Those who claim ignorance of Obama's propensity to murder, are those like Hillary who know it only too well.

Not only has Obama singled out American citizens for execution without trial, a/k/a murder. His undeclared wars in Libya and Syria, and his support for terrorists there, have killed tens of thousands, both directly, and by forcing millions to flee Obama's killers at whatever risk to their own lives, with thousands drowning in the Mediterranean trying to get to Europe.

Obama learned to love murder from his Indonesian stepfather, Lolo Soetoro. Here's how *Newsweek* reporter Jon Meacham quoted Obama in an August 22, 2008 article: "My stepfather was a good man who gave me some things that were very helpful. One of the things that he gave me was a pretty hard-headed assessment of how the world works."

As Brent Bedford wrote in these pages in our May 1, 2015 issue[1], Obama's stepfather was, according to all available evidence, a mass-murderer. When he met Obama's mother, Ann Dunham Obama, in Hawaii in

Barack Obama's Indonesian step-father Lolo Soetoro (left), Ann Dunham (center), and Barack on the right.

1962, the Indonesian Soetoro was already 27 years old and in the Indonesian Army reserve. He was training in Hawaii as a geologist, and met Ann at the East-West Institute. They were married in March of 1965.

Three months later, just in time for the moves by the U.S.-backed military against President Sukarno and his nationalist coalition (which included the Indonesian Communist Party [PKI]), Soetoro was called back to Indonesia, where he held the rank of Lieutenant Colonel. According to available sources, he spent the next months, if not years, in the military, which was carrying out massacres against communists, nationalists, and others, under the command of Gen. Suharto. Estimates of the number killed reach at least 500,000.

Barack and his mother Ann joined Soetoro in Jakarta in 1967, when Obama was six years old, old enough to have memories of his step-father of considerable clinical interest, some of which appear in his autobiographies, and others in various interviews.

Human Rights Watch, in a post on February 21, 2010, pointed to a section of Obama's *Dreams From*

---

1. See *EIR*, May 1, 2015. The article relies heavily on *The Manufacturing of a President: The CIA's Insertion of Barack H. Obama, Jr. into the White House*, by Wayne Madsen.

My Father which records the following conversation between Obama and his stepfather:

A queer notion suddenly sprang into my head.

"Have you ever seen a man killed?" I asked him.

He glanced down, suprised by the question.

"Have you?" I asked again.

"Yes."

"Was it bloody?"

"Yes."

I thought for a moment. "Why was the man killed? The one you saw?"

"Because he was weak."

"That's all?"

Lolo shrugs and rolled his pant leg back down. "That's usually enough. Men take advantage of weakness in other men. They're just like countries in that way. The strong man takes the weak man's land. He makes the weak man work in his field. If the weak man's woman is pretty, the strong man will take her." Lolo paused to take another sip of water, then asked, "Which would you rather be?"

I didn't answer, and Lolo squinted up at the sky. "Better to be strong," he said finally rising to his feet. "If you can't be strong, be clever and make peace with someone who's strong. But always better to be strong yourself. Always."

Lolo finally remarked, "Better to be strong."

Now you must relisten to those words, hearing them this time through the ears of a six-year old.

Now, don't repeat to yourself any longer that it is impossible to remove Obama. Now, it suddenly is possible. After Russian President Putin's flanking maneuver against the terrorists in Syria, members of Obama's own government, including leading members, are working around him and at cross-purposes with him in the interests of peace. Now, precisely now, he can and must be removed under the 25th Amendment for mental unfitness to discharge the duties of President.

Scratch Obama, and you will find Lolo Soetoro's belief that, according to the political editor of the *Chicago Sun-Times*, "a man took on the powers of whatever he ate. One day soon, he promised, he would bring home a piece of tiger meat for us to share."

Zepp-LaRouche Presents *EIR*'s New Silk Road Report at Beijing Symposium

by William Jones

Oct. 3—The Chinese edition of the *EIR* report, "The New Silk Road Becomes the World Land-Bridge" was officially presented by Helga Zepp-LaRouche, the founder of the Schiller Institutes, at a symposium sponsored by the Chongyang Institute for Financial Studies at Renmin University on Sept. 29. The Chongyang Institute is also a co-sponsor of the Chinese-language report.

The Chongyang Institute was established a few years ago by graduates of Renmin University, and fashions itself as the new type of think-tank called for recently by President Xi Jinping, who is concerned about receiving the best analysis of the present world situation and some key recommendations for policy as China and the world enter into a new era of international relations. Wang Wen, the Executive Dean of the Chongyang Institute, as well as Mr. Fu Jianming, the Vice President of the Pheonix Publishing & Media Group which published the Chinese version of the report, made introductory comments at the press conference, which drew 70 people, including at least 15 journalists.

The Genesis of a New Paradigm

In her address to the symposium, Mrs. LaRouche explained her role in the germination of the idea known in China as the "One Belt, One Road" project. She explained how she and her husband, economist and statesman Lyndon LaRouche, had, with the break-up of the Soviet Union, expanded on the series of development programs they had worked on for decades,

RDCY

Helga Zepp-LaRouche speaks at the symposium on "The Belt and Road Initiative of Sino-U.S. Cooperation" & Book Launch of From a Silk Road to a World Land-Bridge *held in Beijing on Sept. 29.*

to elaborate a program for linking the entire Eurasian continent.

This would be done with a system of high-speed rail lines that would help bring the land-locked and newly independent nations of Central Asia, and vast underpopulated and underdeveloped regions of Asiatic Russia, into the mainstream of international commerce and trade, thereby creating a land corridor for trade and economic development between Europe and Asia. The LaRouches dubbed this "The Eurasian Landbridge."

Discussions with representatives of the Chinese government in the early 1990s led to a conference in Beijing organized under the auspices of the Chinese Ministry of Science and Technology in 1996, Mrs. LaRouche explained. This conference with leading experts from China and 34 other Eurasian countries, included an address by Mrs. LaRouche devoted to the implementation of this project. The Asian financial crisis of 1997 and the ruble crisis of 1998 prevented the further movement of this project. And it was only in September 2013 that Chinese President Xi Jinping revived the notion in his famous speech at Nazarbayev University in Kazakhstan, calling for the creation of a Silk Road Economic Belt to unite Europe and Asia.

The concept of the New Silk Road points in the direction of a new paradigm of mankind, Zepp-LaRouche told her audience, and away from the "geopolitics" which caused two world wars in the last century, and calls for replacing it with the idea of the common aims of mankind, which is reflected in Xi Jinping's "win-win policy." While the "One Belt, One Road" has become the going term for the Chinese project, Mrs. LaRouche underlined the importance of the Silk Road precedent. "We should keep the term the New Silk Road," she said, "as it clearly expresses this cultural vision of cooperation manifested by the ancient Silk Road."

She then went into the crisis in the Middle East and the massive flow of refugees into Europe from the wartorn areas created by U.S. policy under Bush and Obama. There is a very recent recognition by many European nations, that there must be a change in policy and the root causes of the refugee crisis must be adressed, she said. It is not enough to fight the Islamic extremists militarily; there must also be a real economic reconstruction of the entire region, which is now completely destroyed by war, to create a future for the young people now being attracted to violent jihad.

"We can extend the Silk Road to the Middle East," she said, "creating centers of development. We can make the deserts bloom and create new cities. The New Silk Road can become a peace order for the Twenty-first Century," she said. "If successful, it will create a new age of civilization, and if it fails, we will enter a new dark age."

Reversing 40 Years of Disaster

EIR's Washington Bureau Chief Bill Jones then outlined the tremendous possibilities opened for the world, including the United States, with the implementation of the Silk Road project. He noted how Lyndon LaRouche, in 1975, proposed the creation of an International Development Bank for financing the development of the

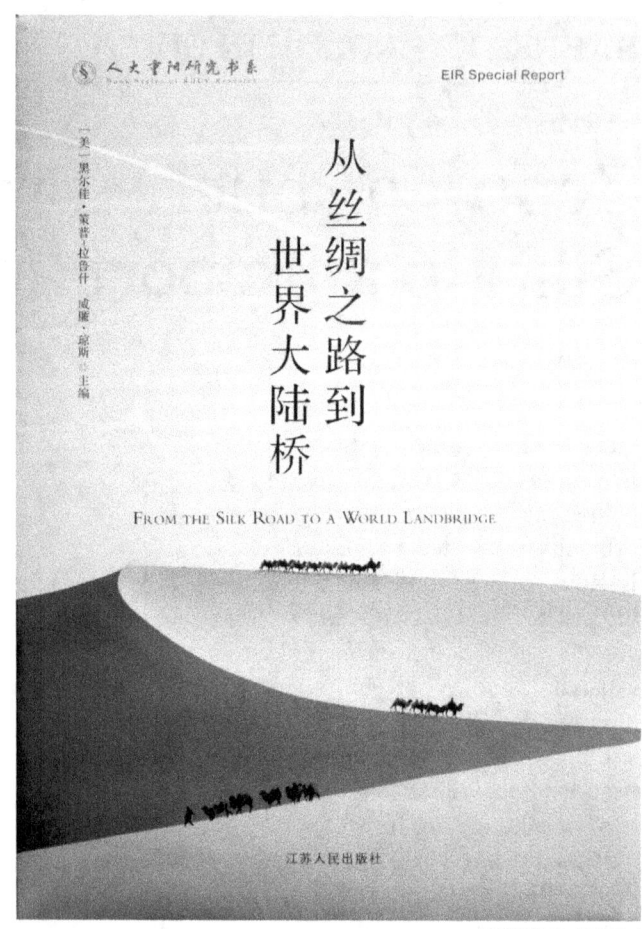

EIRNA/Stefan Tolksdorf

The cover of the newly released Chinese language version of EIR's special report "The New Silk Road Becomes the World Land-Bridge."

Third World, and how the Foreign Minister of Guyana Fred Wills, had, in collaboration with LaRouche, issued at the UN General Assembly in 1976 a call for a New World Economic Order and a debt moratorium for the developing nations.

"But there would be no new world economic order nor any debt moratorium," Jones said. And the world then entered into a new phase of inflationary expansion of the world financial system which now encompasses over two quadrillion dollars of accumulated—and unpayable—debt. "President Xi's project of a land and maritime Silk Road Initiative offers now the possibility of reversing that dangerous trajectory," Jones said. "The world stands in amazement over China's development in the last few decades," Jones said, "and now China is offering a similar development for the rest of the world."

Jones also noted that, while the U.S. Administration

has been less than enthusiastic about the project, there was a growing understanding in the United States, particularly at the state and local levels, which are greatly suffering the effects of the financial crisis, as well as among industrial layers, that what China is doing—and is offering the world—represents a ray of hope in an otherwise disastrous economic situation.

The Appreciation by Experts

These two presentations were followed by comments from eight leading Chinese scholars, who had read the report. Their reaction to the report was absolutely electric. Professor Bao Shixiu, formerly a Professor of Military Strategy at the PLA Academy of Military Sciences, said that bringing together the countries of the region around the New Silk Road initiative in a process of regional development was the task of the day. "It is also related to the notion of good governance," Professor Bao said, "and everyone has good feelings about this concept. We will thereby create a good neighborhood and begin to build a European common destiny." This was also the idea behind the notion of the Eurasian Landbridge put forward by the Schiller Institute in the 1990s, he said.

Ding Yifan, the former deputy director of the World Development Institute of the Development Research Center of the State Council of the PRC, underlined the importance of the economic concepts of Lyndon LaRouche, lying at the basis of the report. "I have known the Schiller Institute for a long time," he said, "and I have learned much from them. They have very specific ideas about the world economy. The concept underlying LaRouche's view of the economy is that of the physical economy. LaRouche used the term negentropy to characterize the underlying laws of a healthy functioning economy," Ding Yifan said.

"Helga Zepp-LaRouche put forward the concept of the Eurasian Landbridge as a war avoidance concept," Ding added. "The new concept of the Belt and Road has received great attention from the whole world. … We cannot allow capital to control everything. Instead, we must control capital."

RDCY

Wang Wen, the Executive Dean of the Chongyang Institute for Financial Studies (RDCY), opened up the Sept. 29 symposium in Beijing.

Shi Ze from the China Institute of International Studies explained how the problem in the world today is caused by geopolitical thinking. "Geopolitics has led to the dangerous situation we have today. The aim of the report is to develop a concept to replace geopolitics. And I found such a concept in this book," Shi said. "On the other hand, is the economic aspect of the report, which places the stress on creating infrastructure. We have to look at the infrastructure needs of the other countries," he said. "I am confident about the development of the Landbridge and I believe Mrs. LaRouche has made great progress in her idea."

Tao Qingmei of the Beijing Long Way Foundation noted that the report also mooted the question of a new order and a new relationship between nations. "This book reflects the views of U.S. experts and I really respect them. We should rethink the world on the basis of the new relationship between nations."

Wang Xiangsui, the director for the Center for Strategic Studies at Beijing University of Aeronautics and Astronautics, called the report "a road to the future." "Today we have to proceed from a regional perspective, one which involves economics, politics, and culture. China is learning from other countries. And this book is very important in that respect," he said.

Zhang Jianping, the Director of the Department of International Economic Cooperation at the National Development and Reform Commission, underlined the collaborative nature of the Silk Road Initiative and its openness to all countries. While noting scepticism from the U.S. side about the Silk Road project, he saw a certain shift in policy with regard to the U.S. view of the AIIB (Asian Infrastructure Investment Bank). Europe, on the other hand, was becoming absolutely enthusiastic about the project. Zhang felt that the *EIR* report, which he also noted was the result of 20 years' labor, was an important element in promoting the idea of the New Silk Road in the United States.

Zhao Changhui from the China Export-Import Bank praised Progress Publishing for bringing out this report. He called the Silk Road project a thousand-year initiative. "When reading the report we have to ask ourselves how we can make a difference. It leads us to reflect on our own obligations." He said that scholars must develop a long-term vision, as it was reflected in the report.

Liu Ying, the Director of the Department of Cooperative Research at Chongyang Institute, noted that the report was written from a global perspective, but from a modern global perspective, including from a space perspective. "This report is about predicting the future rather than just explaining the past," Liu Ying said.

All the participants received a copy of the Chinese report. The Chongyang Institute had purchased 1,000 copies which they will distribute free of charge to a wide section of the Chinese political and intellectual circles. There was a considerable amount of coverage of the press conference in the economic press stressing the fact that this was the first analysis by "American scholars" of the Chinese project. There was also widespread recognition in the media reports of the role of Mrs. LaRouche and the Schiller Institute as a key initiator of this project in the early 1990s.

The high-level participation in the event by eight Chinese scholars, and the sponsorship by the prestigious Chongyang Institute for Financial Studies, underlined the fact that the *EIR* report has now become an authoritative source for Chinese scholars in pursuing the "One Belt, One Road" project. The economic concepts championed by Lyndon LaRouche over the period of 50-plus years have now become a staple for the intellectual layers in this, the most populous country in the world.

In the Face of the Refugee Crisis: Realizing a Grand Vision

by Helga Zepp-LaRouche

Chairman of the German Civil Rights Movement Solidarity political party (BüSo)

Oct. 6—The escalating refugee crisis has split Germany into two fundamentally opposed camps: the majority (as of now) of people who respond as good Samaritans to the distress of the refugees, and actively help in one way or another to alleviate some of this distress. With her statement "We will do it!", Chancellor Merkel expressed the attitude of that majority.

Then there's the other side, which ranges from Christian Social Union head Horst Seehofer, to Interior Minister Thomas de Maizière, to Schäble's son-in-law Thomas Strobl, Bavarian Finance Minister Markus Söder, the Alternative for Germany Party, and the xenophobic Pegida movement.[1] Their common denominator is stoking the fear and resentment of the population and offering proposed "solutions" which ultimately violate human rights, in some cases marked by open racism, all of which share one thing—total inadequacy for solving the problem.

The political climate between these two camps has now become so hot, aggravated by an objective overload on the municipalities and inadequate housing capacities for the refugees, that the situation in Germany is about to become uncontrollable. If it should come to that, this crisis would have fateful consequences for all of Europe, due to the relative weight of Germany on the continent.

This is not a crisis whose end is in sight; on the contrary, on an almost daily basis, streams of incriminating

UNCHR

A Syrian woman and her children, among the lucky ones who made it to the Greek island of Lesbos after crossing the Aegean Sea from Turkey.

pictures come out of bodies of refugees washed up on the Mediterranean coast, among them babies and small children, a mirror-image of the failed EU policy, which has ignored the looming catastrophe for years, and left primarily Greece and Italy to handle it alone. Officially, 2,600 people have drowned this year alone; the number of unreported cases must be much higher. But it's not only desperate Syrians who are risking their lives in the attempt to escape death; millions of people in Afghanistan, Iraq, Yemen, Libya, and many more African countries, or in refugee camps in countries such as in Turkey, see no future, and set off for Europe.

There are some, who, like Frontex director Fabrice Leggeri[2], are demanding that deportation prisons (or

---

1. PEGIDA stands for Patriotic European Against the Islamicization of the Occident. The movement was founded in Dresden, Germany and has been holding anti-Islam demonstrations since October 2014.

2. Frontex is the European Agency for the Management of Operational Cooperation at the External Borders of the Member States of the European Union. It was established in October 2004.

Development Plans for the Middle East and Africa on the Table in 1991

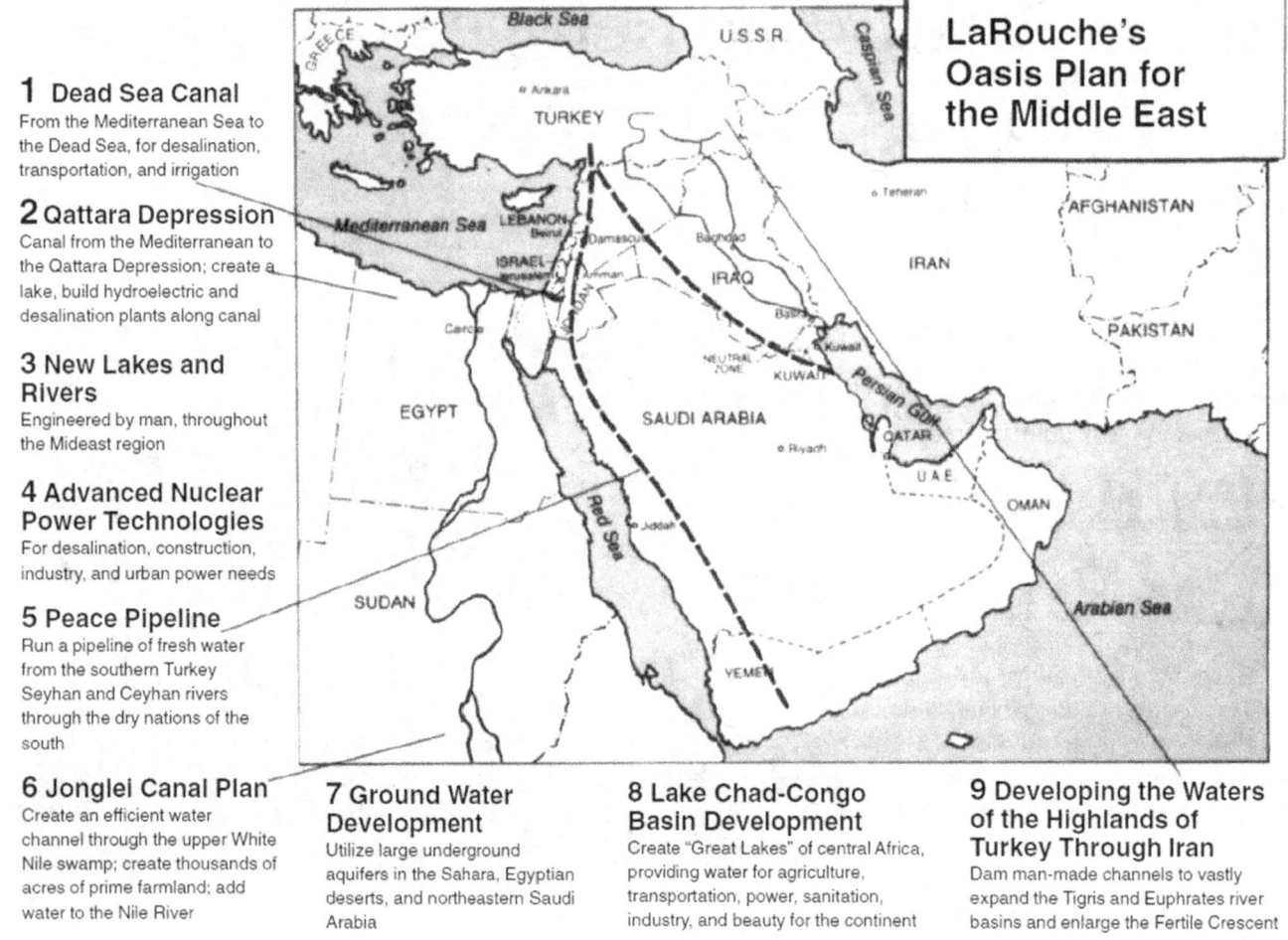

1 Dead Sea Canal
From the Mediterranean Sea to the Dead Sea, for desalination, transportation, and irrigation

2 Qattara Depression
Canal from the Mediterranean to the Qattara Depression; create a lake, build hydroelectric and desalination plants along canal

3 New Lakes and Rivers
Engineered by man, throughout the Mideast region

4 Advanced Nuclear Power Technologies
For desalination, construction, industry, and urban power needs

5 Peace Pipeline
Run a pipeline of fresh water from the southern Turkey Seyhan and Ceyhan rivers through the dry nations of the south

6 Jonglei Canal Plan
Create an efficient water channel through the upper White Nile swamp; create thousands of acres of prime farmland; add water to the Nile River

7 Ground Water Development
Utilize large underground aquifers in the Sahara, Egyptian deserts, and northeastern Saudi Arabia

8 Lake Chad-Congo Basin Development
Create "Great Lakes" of central Africa, providing water for agriculture, transportation, power, sanitation, industry, and beauty for the continent

9 Developing the Waters of the Highlands of Turkey Through Iran
Dam man-made channels to vastly expand the Tigris and Euphrates river basins and enlarge the Fertile Crescent

LaRouche in '92 (published in 1991)

Prior to the escalating wars and terrorist onslaught in the region, these projects proposed by Lyndon LaRouche were all under discussion.

jails) be established in the so-called hotspots of Italy and Greece, in order to prevent the refugees from entering EU territory through its external borders. Others want to deploy Frontex-ships against the traffickers—which obviously puts the lives of the refugees in great danger.

Striking the same tone are proposals like those of Markus Söder to change the Constitution in order to restrict the right of asylum to specific quotas—a clear violation of the Geneva Convention. Human rights organizations also consider the new asylum proposals by Interior Minister de Maizière to be unconstitutional and totally inappropriate for solving the problems in managing the refugee crisis, not least because they increase the panic among the refugees at having Europe's gates shut on them.

It is dawning on some that this refugee migration is in reality a mass migration comparable to the great migrations of late antiquity. They are the result of a decades-long failed policy of the geopolitical wars of Bush and Obama in Southwest Asia, which were based on lies; and of the conditionalities policy of the IMF, which suppressed economic development and created the breeding ground for terrorism through the resulting poverty.

The idea that you could remedy this situation which is totally coming apart at the seams, by building a new Limes Wall around Europe, and declaring the Near East and Africa *terra incognita*,—as is proposed in the 1991 essay by Jean-Christophe Rufin "The Empire and the new Barbarians: North-South Rupture,"—is absurd, and ultimately reflects the moral and political bankruptcy of its advocates. Should pictures of terrorized refugee children shown between NATO barbed wire and tear gas, who are the victims of a failed policy,—should shot refugees and drowned bodies become the "new normal?"

With reference to the xenophobic Pegida demonstrations and the burning refugee shelters, *Die Welt* wrote that Mrs. Merkel could only survive the next two years if she gets the refugee problem under control. A fair assessment, and even more so in view of the fact that the trans-Atlantic financial system can implode at any minute, and the gigantic derivatives bubble evaporate in a super-crash, as, among other things, the Glencore crisis calls to mind. It should be clear to any thinking human being that the chaos which would result from such a crash, would destroy the foundations of society, and scuttle all calculations on the refugee question.

A New Paradigm

There is a way out—but it requires a totally new paradigm and a totally new way of thinking. Only if the military operation by Russia, and now China, in Syria, and possibly Iraq, is followed by a comprehensive economic reconstruction program, that actually develops the Southwest Asian region which has been bombed back into the Stone Age, and permits people there to have the future which they don't have now, can the mass migration be stopped. The same goes for Africa.

Already in 2012, the Schiller Institute worked out an extensive development program for Southern Europe, the Mediterranean region, Southwest Asia and Africa, which was based on earlier development plans. In 2014, the Schiller Institute's associates at the news magazine *EIR*—this magazine—published the report "The New Silk Road Becomes the World Land-Bridge," which includes those development plans.

The basic idea is to develop the whole of Southwest Asia with a comprehensive development program; the greening of the deserts with desalination of large amounts of sea water, and other modern methods of fresh water production, such as ionization of the moisture in the atmosphere, together with the building of integrated infrastructure projects, industry and agriculture, and new cities will totally change the characteristics of the region.

Only if poverty is eliminated, and, most important, young people, and especially young men, are given a real perspective for the future, can the problem of terrorism be overcome. Naturally, the known sources of funding this terrorism—for example, through drug cultivation in Afhganistan and certain Wahhabi "charity" organizations, must be cut off.

It is clear that such a change in paradigm is only feasible if all the major neighbors of the region—Russia, China, India, Iran, Egypt, and the European nations—and hopefully also the United States—work together. To stop mass migration from Southwest Asia and Africa, geopolitics must be shelved, and replaced by the common aims of mankind. Among these aims is victory over terrorism, which threatens Europe, as well as Russia, China, India, and the United States,—and the need to preventing the refugee crisis from shattering the foundations of European society.

In addition to adopting a development perspective, the problem of the integration of those refugees already in Europe must immediately be addressed. In Germany today there are about 45 million employable persons; in 2050 that figure will only be 29 million, and in many other countries the situation is similar. The integration of such a new workforce is therefore in our own fundamental interest.

Why should the young employable refugees not be involved immediately in the construction of a half million units of subsidized housing? The financing could be undertaken by the Reconstruction Finance Bank (Kreditanstalt für Wiederaufbau) just as it financed the German economic miracle after the Second World War, and it would have the same economic effect. The mere announcement of this project, in combination with an extension of the New Silk Road toward Southwest Asia and Africa, would eradicate the current despair and anxiety for the future, and give way to a spirit of optimism.

The mean-spirited skeptics should ask themselves the question: do they really believe that the current policy toward the Middle East and Africa can actually go on forever? On the positive side: With China's policy of the New Silk Road and President Xi Jinping's offer of "win-win" cooperation for building the New Silk Road, we already have the framework in place for the perspective outlined here. The fact that the report "The New Silk Road Becomes the World Land-Bridge" has just been published in Chinese translation, and at the book launch received the enthusiastic support of ten representatives of leading Chinese economic institutes, demonstrates that this perspective presents a realistic opportunity, for which cooperation from Russia, China, and India can be relied upon, to resolve the refugee crisis in a totally new way. That opportunity need only be seized.

Zepp-LaRouche on Chinese TV: Points To New Paradigm Needed Among Nations

Oct. 3—Helga Zepp-LaRouche, founder of the Schiller Institute, was one of three panelists on CCTV's "Dialogue: Ideas Matter" show Sept. 28. The program was moderated by Yang Rui, and included Prof. Jin Canrong of Renmin University of China in the studio with Mrs. LaRouche, and Prof. M.D. Nalapat, the UNESCO Peace Chair at Manipal University in India, by video.

The half-hour discussion was devoted to issues raised at the recent United Nations General Assembly session. We include below the interventions of Mrs. LaRouche.

Helga Zepp-LaRouche during the Sept. 25 panel discussion hosted by CC-TV on the subject of the recent General Assembly of the United Nations.

The Question of Development

Host Yang Rui asked Mrs. LaRouche to comment on President Xi's commitment of $2 billion to poorer nations around the world.

Zepp-LaRouche: Well, I think it has to be seen in the context of the extraordinary speech that he gave at the United Nations, which was the most optimistic, most encouraging speech of all the other leaders in my view, because he emphasized the promised development for the whole world, as part of the 'win-win' policy of China. He emphasized innovation, for example. So, the $2 billion is only like a gesture, in a much broader policy of the 'win-win' policy and the China model which China is offering right now.

Prof. Nalapat noted that China has taken 500 million people out of absolute poverty in the past generation, and has advanced women's rights.

Host Yang Rui asked Mrs. LaRouche if Xi's and Indian Prime Minister Narendra Modi's early personal experiences with poverty affect their policies, and to what extent.

Zepp-LaRouche: I think a lot. And I think both leaders are really exceptional from the standpoint of caring for their people. They both have expressed a tremendous optimism for the future. Modi, for example, has said that the BRICS countries are the first alliance of countries which are not defined by their present capacities, but by the potentials of the future.

And I think both of them, having been poor, and having gone through difficult times—in the case of Xi Jinping, the period of the Cultural Revolution was very difficult....

After some discussion on the refugee crisis internationally, host Yang Rui asked all three panelists about the UN's Millennium Development Goals, which state that poverty is supposed to be cut in half by now, and about the attitude of Pope Francis on the violence of uncontrolled greed. Prof. Nalapat expressed his agreement with the Pope and brought up Bill Clinton's repeal of Glass-Steagall, implying that it led to the 2008 crash and to great income inequality.

Yang then asked Mrs. LaRouche: Is China a "developed" or "developing" country? There is a new level of agreement between China and the United States, including Washington's promises to support the efforts of the AIIB. Will China make big contributions to development of peoples?

Zepp-LaRouche: Oh, I think China has done that already. You see, in the BRICS policy, and the 'win-win' policy of Xi Jinping, China has contributed or taken leadership to create a completely alternative economic model; and that, at a time when the trans-Atlantic financial system is about to blow out in a bigger crash than 2008.

So, I think the whole world has joined the AIIB, for example, because it's the more attractive model, because it's aimed towards real investment, infrastructure, and other aspects of real economy, while the trans-Atlantic world is about to go bankrupt. The European banks are completely bankrupt; Wall Street is more than bankrupt. And since the gentleman from India mentioned Glass-Steagall—there is, right now, a big push in the United States to return to Glass-Steagall, which would mean to bankrupt the bankrupt Wall Street banks. That would be a very good thing.

So it's really a gift from heaven, almost, that China has started to create this alternative system, like a lifeboat at the time the Titanic is sinking.

So, while it is good that there is a better understanding between the United States and China at this moment, that does not solve the problem of the tendency of the United States still being for a unipolar world.

I think that we are in a period of tremendous change. Europe is changing; there is a big response to the refugee crisis, because this has 'popped the bubble' that we are living in a world where wars that start in one part of the world....

Yang concluded: "You're also the author of a report, 'From the Silk Road to World Land-Bridge,' [he shows it], a fantastic, very impressive report."

"You're watching 'Dialogue' with Madam LaRouche, founder of the Schiller Institute, and Prof. Jin Canrong, and Prof. M.D. Nalapat. We are discussing issues of the UN General Assembly in New York."

The Issue of Women's Rights

CCTV host Yang then raised the attacks on China for its record on women's rights, and asks for the views of all the panelists. Mrs. LaRouche spoke after the other panelists:

Zepp-LaRouche: I think the only way that disadvantages of women can be overcome, is if both genders are living a creative existence; because only when each man and woman is fulfilling their creative potential to the fullest, can there be equality.

And in that respect, I think, all over the world, more needs to be done without any question. But I think that China was promoting female Taikonauts—female astronauts—this is a very good sign. We published a book in Germany, where we have on the cover a Chinese female Taikonaut coming back from the spacecraft—completely optimistic.

And that's the kind of role model which is needed. Because you want to have an image where women are in the avant garde of science, and of culture; and I think that that is very good. That's much better than in many parts of the United States....

Representation at the UN Security Council

After a discussion of the demands of numerous countries, including Japan, India, Germany, and Brazil, to have a permanent representative on the UN Security Council, Yang asked Mrs. LaRouche: Should Germany become a Security Council permanent member?

Zepp-LaRouche: I think so, yes, but I think it's a larger issue. Because I think we are at an epochal change, where both geopolitics must be put in the past, and also I don't necessarily agree that the idea of a multi-polar world is so much better than a unipolar world, because it still embodies the idea of geopolitics. I think that as humanity, we have to reach a New Paradigm, where the common aims of mankind are really the focus of the entire human family, and from that standpoint, I think we need a clear representation of all the countries. So I think we must find a modus operandi where Africa is represented, Latin America, Asia, in an appropriate kind of representation.

But I think the key is to have a New Paradigm in which the interests of humanity as a whole, as an immortal species for the future, must guide what every country does. So I think the time where there's a legitimate national interest, or even a legitimate interest of a group of people, against another group of people, must be put aside, and we must define what are the common problems of humanity, which are the elimination of hunger, which is energy security, which is raw materials security.

And I think there again China has taken the lead in their Moon program. The lunar missions of China are really showing the way that science and technology can tackle the problems of raw materials security and energy security. Because China is working towards mining helium-3 on the Moon for a future fusion production finally on the Earth.

I think it's more the question of the vision for the future. It's more the question of how to define the common aims of humanity, and then the representation should reflect that attitude.

Zepp-LaRouche on Chinese Radio: Calls For 'Win-Win' U.S.-China Relations

Sept. 28—Schiller Institute founder Helga Zepp-La-Rouche was interviewed by phone as part of a panel of experts in a 55-minute news discussion of China-Unit3ed States relations on China Radio International News Show on Sept. 25 The show was hosted by Liu Kun and Brian Kopczynski. Other guests included three academic experts in China-U.S. relations: Prof. Tao Wenzhao of the Chinese Academy of Social Science; Prof. Rick Dunham, Tsinghua University, and Prof. Mark Beeson of the University of Western Australia.

China Radio International is the state-owned international radio broadcaster of the People's Republic of China.

United States Must Work with China

The first question was, "What makes the two political giants, China and the U.S., like each other, and what turns them apart?"

Zepp-LaRouche: It is extremely important that the two most important countries in the world in terms of size and power have a stable relationship; the better part of the U.S. is looking at China from that standpoint. On President Xi's part, he has made it very clear that he wants to open up with the 'win-win' policy. However, now, I really think there is a complete disparity right now between how the two countries go about things.

The interviewer noted that "only *USA Today* had a headline on President Xi's visit."

His next question was: "How does China fit into the current global strategy of the U.S., and vice-versa?"

Zepp-LaRouche: I think the various proposals coming from China, which I think are very much based on the Confucian conception that the world can only function if it's based on a harmonious relation among nations, are really the key. This is expressed in President Xi's offer of 'win-win' cooperation; actually, he invited Obama to cooperate with China last year at the APEC [Asia-Pacific Economic Cooperation] meeting on the New Silk Road; on the 'One Belt, One Road' policy, together with the idea of having a new model among major nations.

It's a completely different concept of international relations among nations based on sovereignty, mutual respect, and recognition of different social systems. I think that is the model which is right now very attractive, and which has been adopted by the BRICS [Brazil, Russia, India, China, South Africa] countries; it reaches

White House/Pete Souza

President Obama, second from the left, was the "odd man out" at the Asia-Pacific Economic Cooperation (APEC) conference in November 2014, as he refused to accept Chinese President Xi Jinping's explicit invitation for the U.S. to join the Asian Infrastructure Investment Bank, one of the key institutions of the New Paradigm coming together as a result of Chinese initiatives.

out to ASEAN [Association of Southeast Asian Nations], and also to Ibero-American countries, who enjoy that kind of 'win-win' cooperation with China.

I think, from the Chinese standpoint, the biggest problem and hope, at the same time, would be that the United States responds to that—the offer to the U.S. is still on the table, and I think various Chinese media have repeated that offer: that the Europeans, the United States, and China should cooperate.

I can only hope that the U.S., which is in deep trouble right now—I mean, its financial system is in terrible shape; many people say it's worse than 2008; you could have a major blowout of the financial system at any moment. And the only way the U.S. could get out of it would be if the U.S. would see that chance in that offer right now; you have a major divide: some people see it would be absolutely in the interest of the U.S., and it should cooperate; others say no, we are the only leader in the world—the only major power; Russia is only a regional power, and China should be contained. . . .

Even Joint Chiefs of Staff head Gen. Martin Dempsey [recently succeeded by Gen. Joseph Dunford, Jr.] has warned that the U.S. should not walk into a Thucydides trap and see China as a threat, and try to go to war. And if the U.S. JCS head is warning of that, he must have a good reason.

This dialogue was followed by a discussion of China's economy by the three professors, with Prof. Dunham saying, "It concerns me a bit, that the U.S. decided not to take part in the AIIB [Asian Infrastructure Investment Bank], and is instead pushing the competing idea of the TPP [Trans-Pacific Partnership]." Prof. Tao noted that many Americans, Henry Kissinger included, welcome the AIIB, and criticize Obama for not joining.

The interviewer asked Zepp-LaRouche, "Can economic and trade links still function as the main stabilizer of the bedrock overall relations between the U.S. and China?"

Zepp-LaRouche: I think absolutely, yes. If there are strong economic ties, that is a way to overcome all the present tensions. Of all the deals, I would emphasize that the U.S. and China have agreed to build a fast train between Los Angeles and Las Vegas; it is not my favorite route, because it goes to a casino, but the fact China is providing its very, very advanced technology of advanced trains—for which 18,000 kilometers of track has been built inside China; they are of excellent quality. Everybody knows that the infrastructure of the U.S. needs urgent improvement; the roads, and there is no functional train system.

I have proposed that the U.S. take up the 'win-win' offer. There could be cooperation for developing the train system of the entire U.S. Why not build these from the West to the East Coast, and on the East Coast? They would be far superior to airplanes. If the U.S. would just join the New Silk Road initiative, it would mean the U.S. could be rebuilt.

We Need Productive, Not Monetarist, Values

The professors then discussed the Chinese economy's decline, citing a statistic from Moody's Analytics that for every 1% drop in the Chinese economy, U.S. growth drops .2%, as exemplifying its ripple effect on the world.

Zepp-LaRouche: I would like to comment on this. There is a very big difference, because the U.S. economy is mainly asset-driven—very much asset-driven; very much Wall Street; very much monetarist values, where the Chinese economy for the most part is based on real economy. China has incredible industrial growth; it is engaged in industrial projects with countries around the world.

So even if there was a little problem with the stock market in China, it is much less significant. Wall Street is absolutely bankrupt. I would not compare these two economies in this way. The reality is that Wall Street is absolutely bankrupt. The real economy in the U.S. is in absolutely terrible condition. The fact that the Chinese economy has started to branch out to many parts of the world gives the Chinese economy more substance and validity.

The final question to Zepp-LaRouche was "What can be expected to be accomplished in this trip between these two leaders?"

Zepp-LaRouche: I have written an appeal to the political leaders who will address the UN General Assembly in the next few days, that they should not miss possibly the last opportunity to create a New Paradigm for the world. We have so many problems; we have the danger of a financial blowout; war, terrorism, the refugee crisis in Europe, which is really getting out of control, so I think we need a new era of civilization. And I think the 'win-win' offer of President Xi is the best model on the agenda for that.